Exercise Book for Young Violinists Based on the Mothe

STEP BY STEP

An Introduction to Successful Practice

Volume 2B

Translated from the German Edition "Schritt für Schritt" by Mike Hoover

Photography German Suzuki Institute and Joachim Preuss

Accompanying Play-Along Recording

STEP BY STEP

Rudolf Gaehler, Violin

Kerstin Wartberg, Violin

Kathrin Averdung, Violin

Gino Romero Ramirez, Djembé (African Drum)

David Andruss, Piano

and

Piano Arrangements for All Recorded Pieces

Ingo Klatt, Sound Engineer

Recorded in the Steinway-Haus Heinersdorff, Düsseldorf, Germany

Stream or download the audio content for this book.
To access, visit: **alfred.com/redeem**

Enter the following code: 00-25869_772299

© 2006 Summy-Birchard Music, division of Summy-Birchard Inc.
All rights reserved Printed in USA

ISBN 10: 0-7390-4222-X
ISBN 13: 978-0-7390-4222-9

Summy-Birchard Inc., exclusively administered by
Alfred Music

Practice Plan

Theme this week:

Date:		1st day of practice	2nd day of practice	3rd day of practice	4th day of practice	5th day of practice	6th day of practice
2.	**Warm-up Exercise 1:** *finger pattern exercises (p. 15)*						
	Warm-up Exercise 2: *Let Us All Be Happy Now (p. 16)*						
	Warm-up Exercise 3: *The Bell Songs (p. 18)*						
	Warm-up Exercise 4:						
2.	**Violin Gymnastics with Music:**						
3.	**Exercises for your New Piece:**						
	New Piece:						
4.	**Review Piece with Specific Task:**						
	Other Review Pieces:						
5.	**Concert Piece:**						
6.	**Note-reading:**						

Place an X in the relevant box if you have practiced the task. How many X's will your practice plan have this week?

Contents for this Book and the Companion Recording

Gavotte, *J.B. Lully* — Page 38-45

Minuet, *L. van Beethoven* — Page 46-53

Minuet, *L. Boccherini* — Page 54-61

III. Appendix

> 🔔 = Symbol for additional Warm-Up Exercises

Dear Parents and Colleagues!

Your children and students have once again progressed to the next level. A new book with many beautiful pieces and entertaining, instructional exercises awaits you. Because these are now getting longer and more challenging, and new techniques must be prepared and learned, the division of practice and lesson time into different areas becomes increasingly important.

The contents of this book clearly show that learning occurs on three different levels:

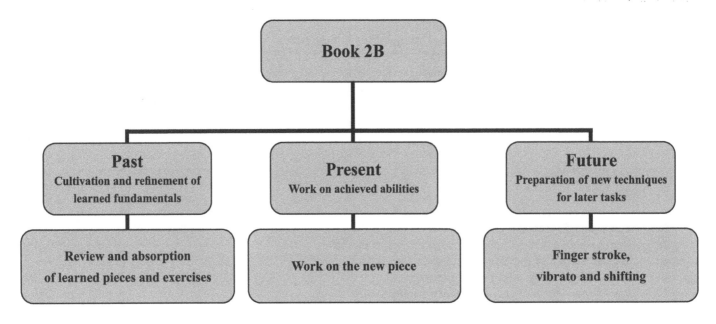

The effective organization of practice and lesson times is just as significant as how much time the child spends practicing. It is very important, however, that none of the learning levels mentioned above be left out. All three complement one another and provide methodical support for an ongoing technical and musical development.

The allotment of time to the different practice areas can be flexibly managed. For example, preparation for a workshop or concert will require more time to be spent on the pieces to be performed. During such times, the normal practice routine can be reorganized, creating an environment for maximizing instructive opportunities. A framework that is too rigid will not provide the opportunity to manage and form necessary practice variations.

The article "Progress Through Repetition" at the end of this book, discusses this most important area of practice, an area which unfortunately receives seldom enough attention.

Book 2B begins with violin gymnastics and warm-up exercises, on which I want to make the following comments:

Violin Gymnastics with Music

This book also begins with many new movement exercises, each illustrated with a photograph. The student should perform these while listening to the piece being learned. At this stage, the finger extension exercise and the preparatory exercises for vibrato should receive most attention. We want to develop flexibility and elegance in these movements, both left and right.

Learning vibrato and to bow with the fingers requires many months of practice. That is why we want to begin preparing these skills already at this stage.

Finger Extension Exercise

This movement (bending and straightening the finger joints) is vital for the further development of tone. The famous violin pedagogue, *Carl Flesch* (1873-1944) writes in his *Urstudien (Basic Studies for Violin)*: "Of all the parts of the right arm, only the fingers come in direct contact with the bow and are the means by which we transmit our most subtle intentions to the strings. Isn't it obvious that the finger joints of the right hand must be considerably more flexible than all the other parts of the arm? Unfortunately, it is precisely these joints that are often entirely neglected ... This is inexcusable." I think he would have been pleased to find the finger extension exercise in this book, as well as the encouragement to practice it often.

Vibrato Exercises

The vibrato exercises introduced here encourage the development of both the arm and wrist vibrato and will train free and relaxed movement of the forearm, wrist and finger joints. After several weeks, the teacher will discover which type of vibrato is easiest for the student and then put emphasis on work in that direction. In any case, free movement of all previously named body parts is necessary for both vibrato types.

We will wait for the next book (3A) to actually attempt the execution of an audible vibrato motion. Then, "The Little Ghost" will sing his song of lamentation, "*Hoohoo hoohoo, hehe hehe, hoo !*"

The Four Finger Patterns

We ended Book 2A with finger-pattern exercises and games. In this book we will pick up where we left off.

In Book 2A, the confident spatial differentiation between the different finger patterns was the main point of emphasis. Now we will occupy ourselves with the feel of the finger patterns as well as the conscious hearing and differentiation of whole and half tones.

The finger pattern exercises begin on the D string, as it is easy for children to sing pitches in this range. These tone sequences are appropriate as warm-up exercises for daily practice as well as for individual and group lessons. They should accompany students for several months until they can sing and play all four finger patterns in tune. Practice suggestions can be found on page 15.

Tone Exercises

The Bell Songs (G major and G minor) and the three-part song "Let Us All Be Happy Now" are meant to provide an instinctive connection between movement and tone.

In this manner students develop an intuitive understanding of pure intonation and a free tone with plenty of resonance. Dr. Suzuki dedicated an entire book to this task using the name "tonalization". This is a word created by imitating the term "vocalization," which is used by singers to describe their tone exercises.

Dear parents and colleagues, concerning tone production I want to share something that Suzuki often said to his students:

Tone is an expression of the living soul.

If this thought is brought to life, work with our students will surpass basic instrumental instruction and reach a much higher dimension.

Violin Gymnastics with Music

Dear young violinist! I welcome you heartily to Book 2B! To help your fingers, hands and arms prepare for the new challenges in this book, we will add new movement exercises to those which we already learned in Book 2A.

To really get into the groove, you should sing or listen to the recording as you perform these exercises and move in rhythm to the music.

Don't forget to review the most important exercises from Book 2A frequently as well:

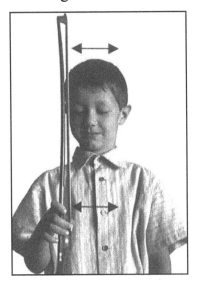  

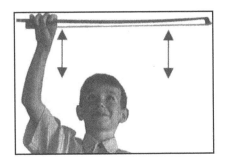 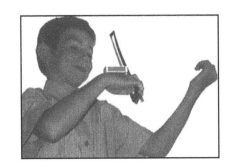 

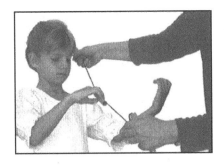  

On the following pages you will find new movement exercises. They will help you to hold your bow with more strength, stability and, at the same time, more flexibility. Later, you will also learn further exercises to prepare your arm, hand and fingers for vibrato.

Always begin new exercises with just a few repetitions, then slowly increase the duration until you can perform the exercise for about one minute. Every exercise should end with a relaxed shaking of the hands and arms before proceeding to the next exercise.

Have fun doing your violin gymnastics!

1. Finger Extension Exercise

This will be one of the most important bow exercises in Books 2, 3 and 4. At first, your fingers will probably experience great difficulty with this exercise, but with persistence and patience you will certainly master it.

Hold a pencil vertically with a beautiful bow hold and stretch your thumb and fingers downward. With this movement, the pencil will move about one-half inch (1 ½ centimeters) downward.

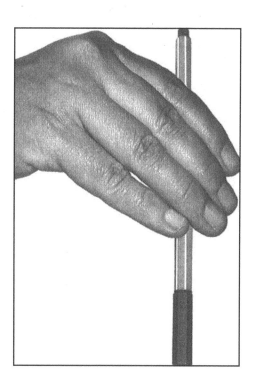

Practice this exercise in three different ways:

1. in the beginning with a pencil;
2. later with the bow, holding it at the balance point;
3. and finally holding the bow at the frog.

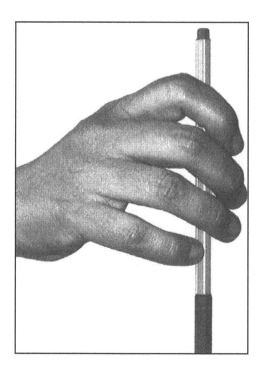

Now return to the starting position. The pencil or bow now moves upward. The thumb is again clearly bent.

Begin the exercise again:

DOWN (= extended fingers)
UP   (= normal, curved fingers)

DOWN – UP – DOWN …

How many repetitions can you perform in one minute? At first, 10 or 15 times will be very respectable. Later, you might manage 100 repetitions per minute!

In Japan, many children practice this motion 10,000 times, but naturally spread out over several months. In their lessons, they show their teachers a calendar on which the number of repetitions is entered for each day. Here is a table representing 30 days. What will your total be?

30 Days Finger Extension Exercise (1 minute daily)										
1	2	3	4	5	6	7	8	9	10	Days 1-10:
11	12	13	14	15	16	17	18	19	20	Days 11-20:
21	22	23	24	25	26	27	28	29	30	Days 21-30:

Total:

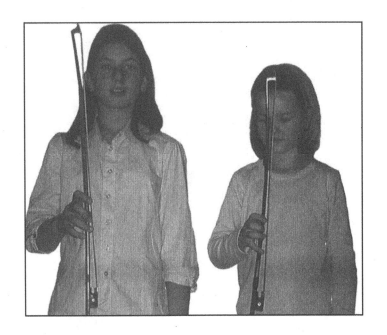

2. The Bow Crawl

On your mark! Get set! Go!

Who will reach the tip first? Crawl with the fingers up the bow stick to the tip and back again down to the frog. The fingers should move like spider legs and are not allowed to touch the bow hair or let the stick slide between them.

3. Finger Tap Exercise

After the Bow Crawl, your fingers will need a chance to relax. Tap each finger of the bow hand on the stick in rhythm with the music. Stiff, sluggish fingers will be revitalized.

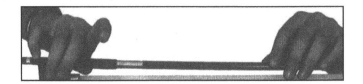

Preparatory exercises for vibrato without the instrument

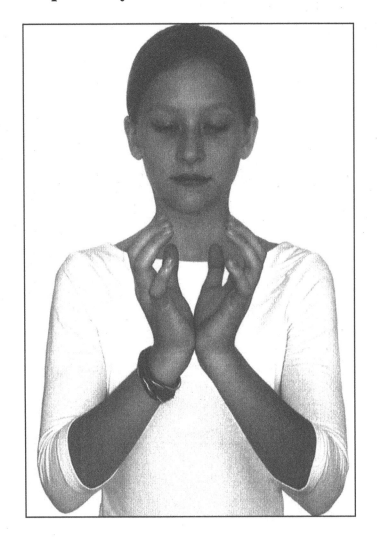

Some of the following exercises teach vibrato motion with the fingers, others with the forearm.

4. Goblet Exercise

Hold your hands as if you are going to pray. Now open your hands – your wrists should remain together – and tap your fingertips together so that you can clearly hear the tapping. Tap various rhythms.

Can the tapping also be heard farther away?

5. The Tic-Tac Exercise

Hold a *Tic-Tac* container in your left hand, then bring your hand into position to play on your magic violin. Now, shake the container towards and away from you approximately ½ to 1 inch (1-2 centimeters). Be sure your head is turned to the left and that your left hand is about as high as your nose.

With the wrist

With the forearm

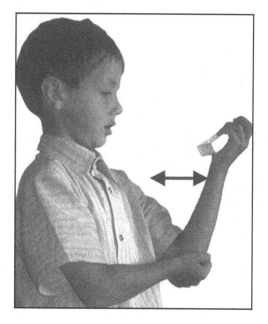

You will hear a rhythmical rattle from the container.

The motion should be carried out first with the wrist, then with the forearm.

Three practice suggestions:

♦ Try to maintain an even rhythm. Count along to determine how long you can do this: Two, three, or four beats in a row? That would be exceptional at this stage!
♦ Perform this exercise with various rhythms.
♦ Begin with a slow, regular tempo and gradually get faster and faster. Use both your eyes and your ears to monitor your progress.

Now something challenging for the finale: As you shake with the left hand, move your right hand as if bowing on your magic violin. It usually requires lots and lots of practice before you can perform two such different motions **simultaneously**.

6. Vibrating Bow Exercise

Your teacher (or mom or dad) should stand behind your right shoulder and hold your bow with the hair pointing up. You should lay the left-hand fingertips on the bow stick and let your arm hang relaxed. Now your teacher can carefully move the bow to provide you with the feeling of a relaxed vibrato motion.

7. Hitchhiker Exercise

For this exercise, your left thumb should point upward as if you want to catch a ride (photo 1).

Now your right hand joins in and holds onto the left thumb.

With your left hand you should begin to wave in a regular rhythm.

Your hand should produce a slight breeze, like a fan. (photo 2)

photo 1

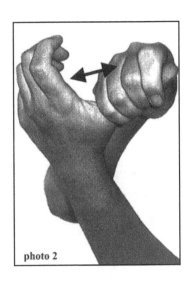

photo 2

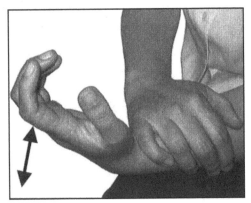

8. Thigh Exercise

Waving motion with the wrist
Lay your left forearm on your left thigh and wave with your wrist (see photo).

Waving motion with the forearm
Brace your left elbow on your left thigh and wave with the forearm.

9. Back of the Hand Exercise

Lay your left thumb onto your right palm (left photograph).

Now lift your hands in front of your face and place the left second or third finger-tip onto the back of the right hand (right photograph).

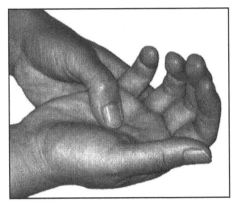

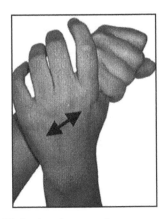

Roll the second or third finger tip back and forth on the back of the right hand. This is almost the same motion that you will need for vibrato.

- ♦ Try performing this exercise without involvement of the thumb. Only the second or third finger-tip should touch the hand. The thumb should remain in the air.
- ♦ Can you roll the finger very slowly at first and then gradually increase the tempo?

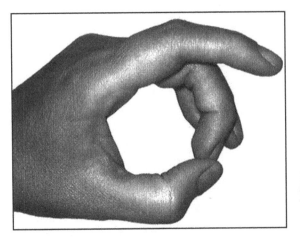

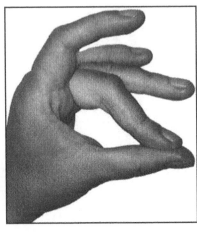

10. Exercise for the distal finger joint

Form a circle with your left thumb and one finger (left photograph). Now extend the thumb and hyperextend the distal finger joint.

Speak as you do this:
round – long – round....

Preparatory exercises with the violin (without the bow)

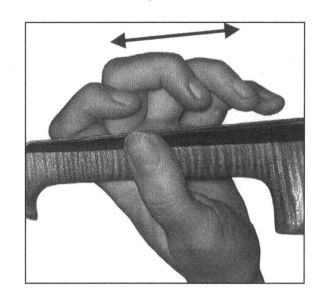

11. Polishing Exercise

Your left hand should be roughly in the second or third position. Now glide up and down the violin neck in three different ways:

a) With the entire hand but **without** fingers on the string: the hand should contact the neck with the middle thumb joint and the side of the knuckle of the first finger.

By the way, this is also a good preparatory exercise for shifting, which you will also be learning soon.

b) With the entire hand, this time **with** fingers on the string: points of contact should be the finger tip and the middle joint of the thumb. The knuckle of the first finger should move away from the neck.

To make this exercise more interesting, you might place a small cloth or tissue beneath your finger tip. Now you will really clean your violin.

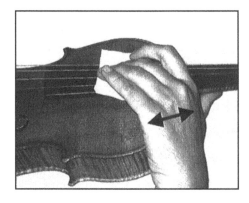

c) With the second and third fingers alone, **without** moving the thumb, which should remain in its normal position on the violin neck. Contact points are again the finger tips and the middle joint of the thumb. The knuckle of the first finger should not touch the neck.

Slide your hand to the middle of the fingerboard and perform the sliding motion here, as demonstrated in the photograph.

12. Waving Exercise No. 1

Lean your hand on the body of the violin and try to wave to yourself vigorously.

The waving motion should come from the **wrist.**

Do you feel the breeze on your nose? This demonstrates that you have performed this exercise correctly.

13. Scroll Exercise

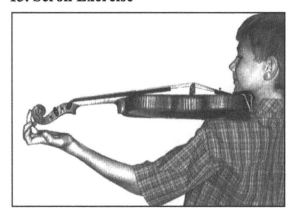

The fingertip of the second or third finger should be placed on the scroll and the student should try to perform a waving motion.

This exercise promotes the arm vibrato.

14. End-of-the-String Exercise

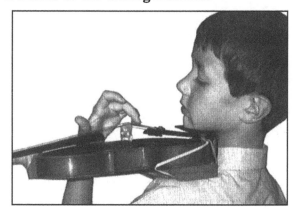

Lay one of your fingertips lightly on the string between the bridge and the tailpiece. Now, try to perform a vibrato motion in this unusual place.

This exercise also promotes the arm vibrato.

15. Waving Exercise No. 2

Place the violin on your shoulder and hold your left hand **to the right** of the neck. Wave to yourself. You can

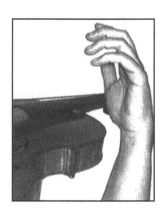

♦ begin slowly and rhythmically, then gradually get faster and faster
♦ wave to yourself with different rhythms.

These motions can be performed equally well with the wrist or with the forearm.

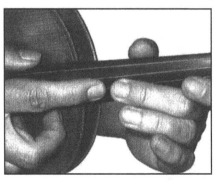

16. Wall Exercise

With your violin in playing position, lean the scroll against the wall. Now you will find the vibrato motion to be much easier.

Vibrate at first with either the second or third finger. Remember that the knuckle of the first finger should not touch the neck of the violin.

17. Roll or "Kiss" Exercise in guitar position

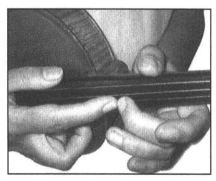

Hold your violin like a guitar and pay careful attention to how your second or third finger roll slowly on the tip.

The motion of the distal finger joint is extremely important. Begin with your finger very flat on the fingerboard. Now place the right index finger close to, but not touching, the left finger. With each rolling motion of the left hand finger, the fingers should "kiss" (= touch). In this way, you can exactly control the rhythm of the motion. Strive for gentle, flowing, circular motions that don't get hung up. Sing the Theme from *Twinkle* and let your fingers "kiss" one, two, three or four times per beat.

The Four Finger Patterns

Having completed Book 2A, you have learned to place your fingers accurately in four finger patterns. Now you will learn to distinguish between them using only your ears. Naturally, this is much more difficult. But if you practice the following short exercises carefully and regularly you will gain much confidence with your intonation.

1. *Sing* all finger pattern exercises with the recording while fingering silently on your violin.

2. *Finger* silently in measures one and two, then play along in measures three to five.

3. *Listen* to the first two measures, then play along to the end. Did you play the correct finger pattern?

4. *Close your eyes* and decide which finger pattern your mom or dad plays from the recording.

5. *Pluck* the open D string *and sing* the different finger patterns without help from the instrument or the recording.

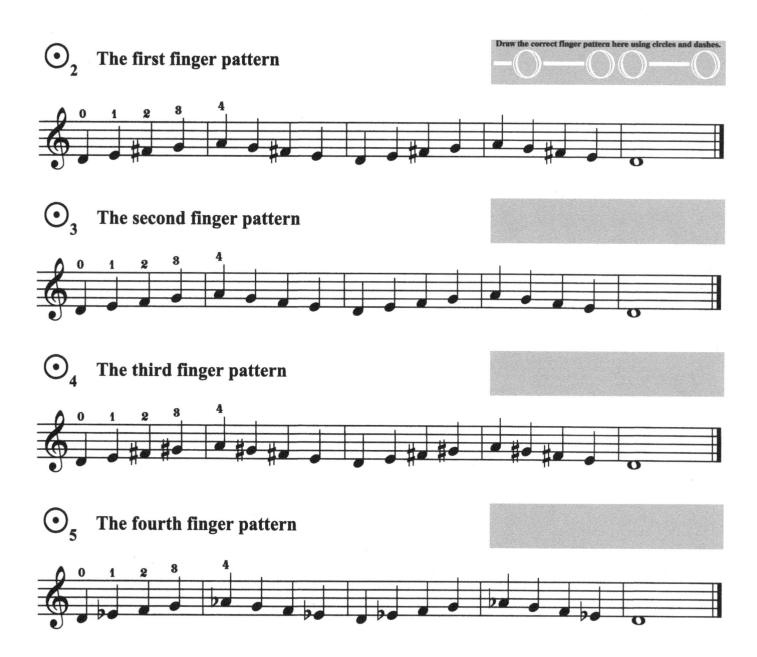

The first finger pattern

The second finger pattern

The third finger pattern

The fourth finger pattern

Tone Exercises

During the next few weeks, always begin your daily practice with *Let Us All Be Happy Now* and *The Bell Song*. Play these pieces with a warm, full tone.

⊙₆ **Let Us All Be Happy Now**   *K. Wartberg*

This song can be sung, or it can be played by three violins. The second and third violin parts are very easy to learn. When your tone is resonant like a bell, it will sound almost as full and beautiful as a small orchestra.

⊙₇ **The Bell Song (Tonalization) in G Major**

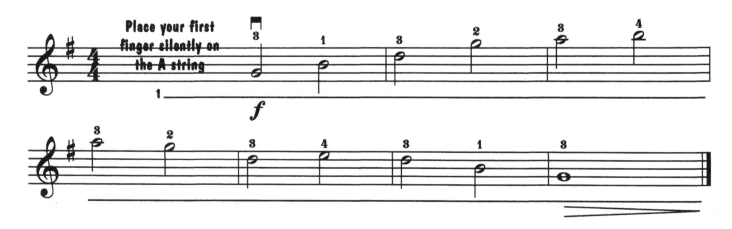

⊙₈ **The Bell Song (Tonalization) in G Minor**

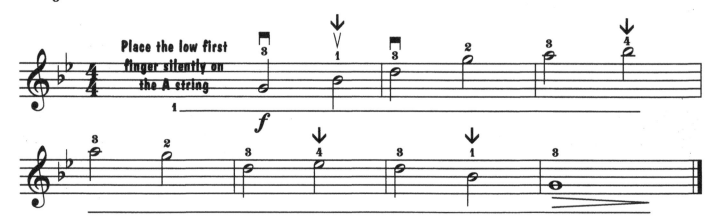

Theme from "Witches' Dance"

⊙₉   **Your new piece – "Witches' Dance"**

Listen regularly to "Witches' Dance" and try some new exercises from the violin gymnastics section.

Practice Suggestion!

Begin first with the preparatory exercises for the fast passage at the end of the piece (tracks 13 and 14). This passage will need lots of practice before it really grooves, so it makes sense to prepare ahead. Now you can begin with the following exercises for the beginning of the piece.

The bow scheme for the beginning on the open E string

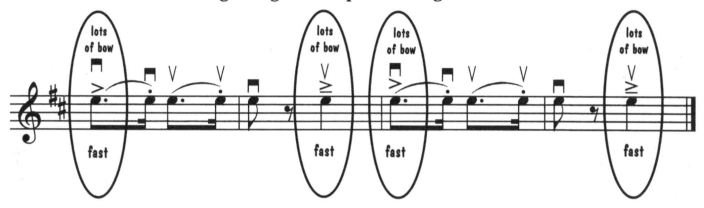

Articulation symbols

> = This symbol is called an accent. Use a rapid bow speed.

> = This symbol means: Bow quickly but broadly.

Preparatory exercise for measures 3 and 4

After the open E string, at the word **STOP**, place your first, second and third fingers with lightning speed on the A string using the third finger-pattern.

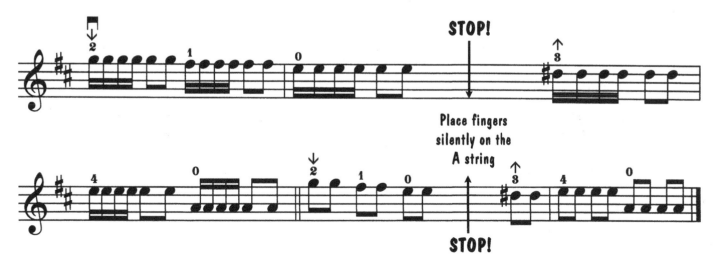

19

The first eight measures

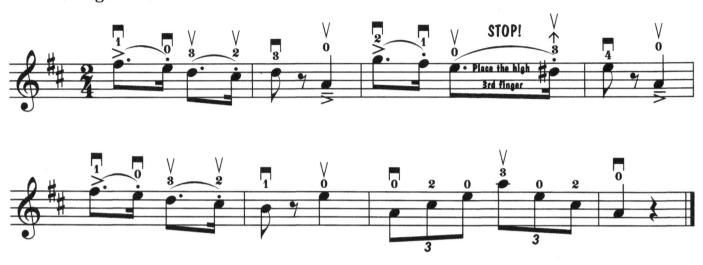

The five important arpeggios in "Witches' Dance"

Practice Suggestions for the quick arpeggios

Practice each short exercise several times. Concentrate on only one of the following points each time:

1. **Good intonation.** Play very slowly and listen closely to whether your intonation is correct.

2. **Small, compact string crossings**. Place your bow on the string almost as if you want to play a double stop, nearly touching the next string to be played. Now you need only a very tiny motion to rock the bow to the other string.

3. **Gradually increase the tempo,** but only when you can play all notes exactly in tune.

Measures 1-24 in a slow practice tempo

◆ **Listen** carefully to the piece and **bow along in the air.** Pay special attention to the rhythm.

◆ **Finger along silently** and take care to place the fingers exactly in their correct places.

◆ **Play** the section with the bow, paying careful attention to rhythmic exactness, short versus long strokes, and fast versus slow bow strokes.

Preparation for the middle section (measures 23-26)

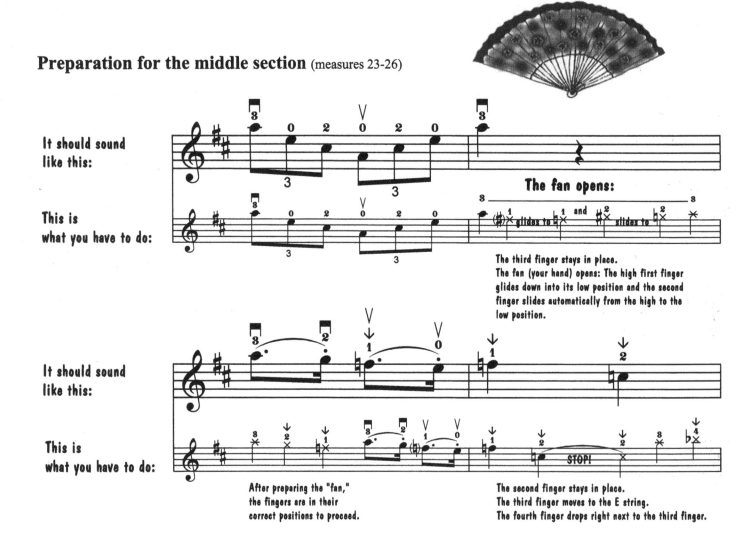

It should sound like this:

This is what you have to do:

The fan opens:

The third finger stays in place.
The fan (your hand) opens: The high first finger glides down into its low position and the second finger slides automatically from the high to the low position.

It should sound like this:

This is what you have to do:

After preparing the "fan," the fingers are in their correct positions to proceed.

The second finger stays in place.
The third finger moves to the E string.
The fourth finger drops right next to the third finger.

The next five measures of the middle section (measures 27-31)

It should sound like this:

This is what you have to do:

The previous preparation has brought the fingers into their correct positions.

Slide the low first finger up next to the second finger.

As you play the third finger, slide the high first finger back to its low position.

It should sound like this:

This is what you have to do:

The high second finger needs no preparation. It falls naturally into place.

⊙ 11 **Measures 25-31 in a slow practice tempo**

Before you begin to play:

Place your first, second and third fingers on the E string using the first finger pattern. During the piano introduction, open your "fan" (hand) to move your fingers into the fourth finger pattern.

Now your fingers are in their proper places and you can begin to play:

Place your fingers very carefully on the string. Where the fingers change to a new finger pattern, always stop and prepare the fingers **before** your bow begins to move.

> **This principle has guided our practice since the very first pieces:** LEFT before RIGHT.

⊙ 12 **Measures 32-41 in a slow practice tempo**

> **A small tip concerning the practic order**

1. Begin by playing only the short transition measure three times.
2. Next, play from the transition measure to the end three times.
3. Now you should play the entire section three times.

If you practice as described above and also frequently play the following two exercises, you will certainly master this section within a few days.

Two triplet exercises with slurs

⊙₁₃ The last four measures with **STOP** after each triplet group

Drum: Violin:

Ram ta ta **STOP!** Ram ta ta   Ram ta ta   Ram ta ta

Ram ta ta   Ram ta ta   Ram ta ta

⊙₁₄ The last four measures with **STOP** after every second triplet group

Drum: Violin:

Ram ta ta Ram ta ta **STOP!**   Ram ta ta Ram ta ta

Ram ta ta Ram ta ta   Ram ta ta Ram ta ta

24

15. "Witches' Dance" – in a medium practice tempo
16. "Witches' Dance" – in performance tempo

N. Paganini

On the recording you can hear a butterfly (violin) and an elephant (drum).

The butterfly flutters its wings two times with lightning speed, then stops abruptly on the upper finger (note with the cross head).

While the elephant stamps twice with his strong leg, the butterfly prepares to flutter again.

Gavotte from "Mignon"

⊙ **18**   **Your new piece - Gavotte from "Mignon"**

Listen to your new piece frequently and learn more exercises in the violin gymnastics section.

Practice tip for the B-flat major section

Prepare yourself for this really tricky section with the following pieces:
- Review the B-flat major scale, The Woodpecker, from Book 2A, Track 16.
- Play one of the following pieces from Book 1 each day, but now in B-flat major. Begin with the low first finger on the A string: Twinkle; Song of the Wind; May Song; Long, Long Ago.

The bow scheme for the beginning of the theme on the open A string

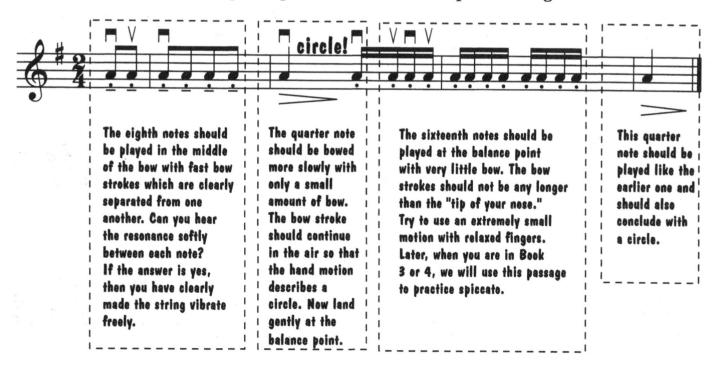

The eighth notes should be played in the middle of the bow with fast bow strokes which are clearly separated from one another. Can you hear the resonance softly between each note? If the answer is yes, then you have clearly made the string vibrate freely.

The quarter note should be bowed more slowly with only a small amount of bow. The bow stroke should continue in the air so that the hand motion describes a circle. Now land gently at the balance point.

The sixteenth notes should be played at the balance point with very little bow. The bow strokes should not be any longer than the "tip of your nose." Try to use an extremely small motion with relaxed fingers. Later, when you are in Book 3 or 4, we will use this passage to practice spiccato.

This quarter note should be played like the earlier one and should also conclude with a circle.

The beginning with the proper notes

Now play the beginning of the theme with the proper notes and continue with one of the three dexterity exercises.

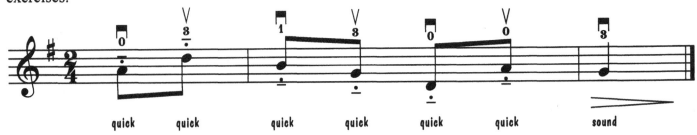

Three short dexterity exercises for the sixteenth note passage

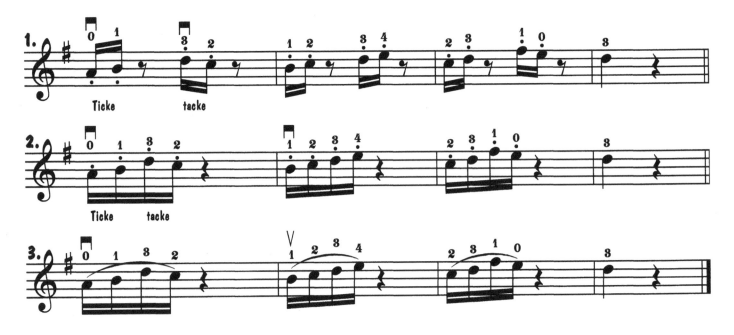

Trill preparation without the bow

Place the first finger on the E string and tap firmly with the low second finger.

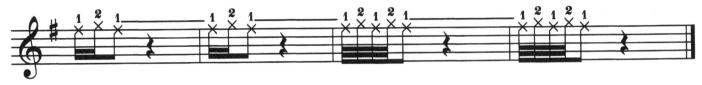

Trill preparation with the bow

Begin each bow stroke with a clear accent. The fast motion of the right hand will automatically influence the left hand, helping your trill to become faster and clearer.

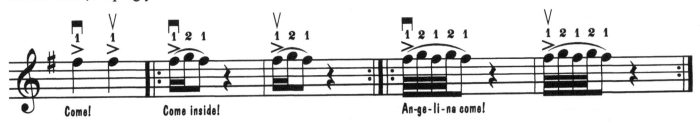

The trill passage in Gavotte

Note for teachers and parents

On the right you will find the above measures from the "Gavotte" as they were originally written. In this

book we use the version that can be found in the Suzuki Violin School. The rhythmical notation for this trill passage demonstrates how systematically this subject is treated in Book 2B:

1.   Tapping the next higher neighboring note once, as in the scale exercise "Butterfly and Elephant"

2.   Tapping the next higher neighboring note twice, as in Gavotte from "Mignon" by Thomas

3.   First real trill in Gavotte by Lully

4.   Trill with a grace note in the Minuet by Boccherini

In Gavotte from "Mignon" rhythmic exactness in execution of the trill should not be the main emphasis.

At this stage it is important

♦   that the finger taps twice within the given time
♦   that the bow stops clearly after the trill
♦   that the bow and fingers move from the E to the A string with lightning speed.

Sliding exercise for the first finger

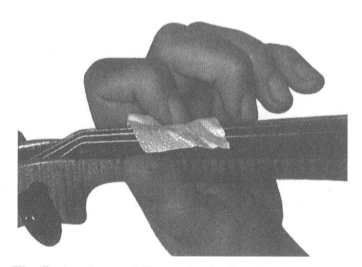

The first and second fingers in the first finger pattern

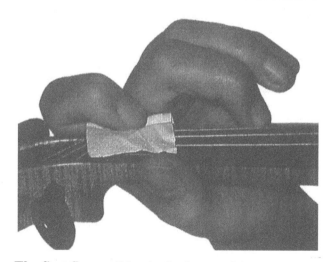

The first finger slides to the low position

Cut a small stripe from a facial tissue. Place the first and second fingers on the A or E string and place the tissue stripe under your first finger. Gently slide the first finger towards the nut and back again to its starting position.

Your second finger, thumb and wrist should not change their positions as you perform this exercise. Do you feel the wide space between the low first and high second fingers? Now you are ready to begin with the preparatory exercises for measures 22 and 23.

Preparatory exercises for the difficult tone progression in measures 22 and 23

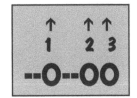

The tone progression using the first finger pattern

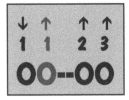

The tone progression after the backward extension of the first finger to the low position

Measures 22 and 23 with the difficult tone progression

A memory aid for the sixteenth note passage in measures 24-27

Transition:

Give a little emphasis to the first note in each group of sixteenth notes. This helps to prevent you from losing your place. Count three groups of four notes two times. After counting the first three groups, the first finger changes its position. A similar strategy should be used in measures 43-46. When you have clearly grasped this concept, you will not find these passages difficult anymore!

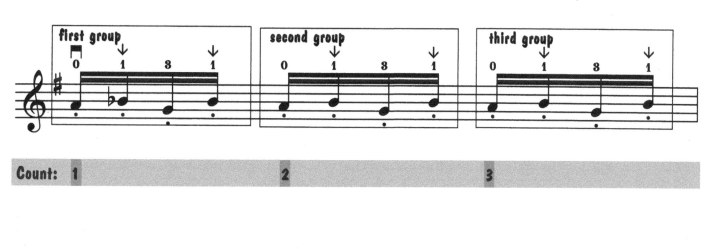

Count: 1   2   3

Count: 1   2   3

⊙₁₉ **Measures 1-35 in a slow practice tempo**

⊙₂₀ The B-flat major section in a slow practice tempo

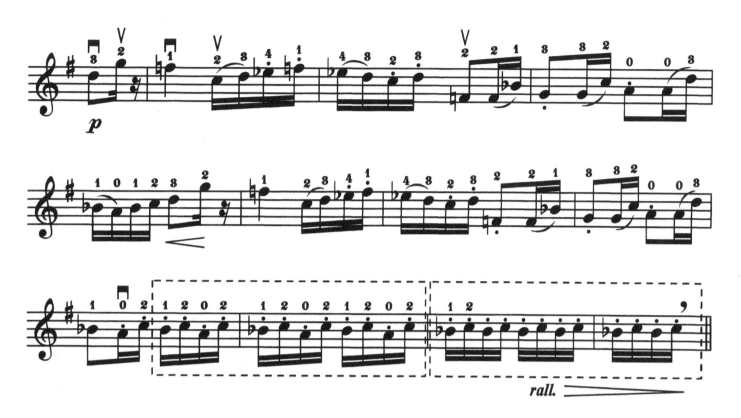

The pizzicato chords at the end

Pluck with your right index finger near the end of the fingerboard, never on the section of the string where you bow! These chords sound best when you pluck with a fast motion using the entire arm. You also need to pay attention that your left fingers press more firmly on the strings for these chords.

⊙₂₁ Measures 66-71 in a slow practice tempo

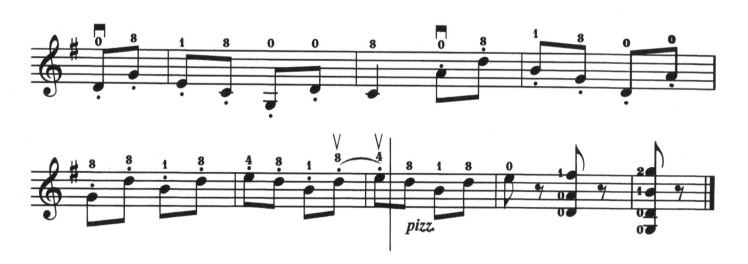

A. Thomas

Three preparatory exercises for the Hungarian Song

1. Extension of the fourth finger upward

As you listen to the "Hungarian Song," perform these sliding exercises with the fourth and first fingers.

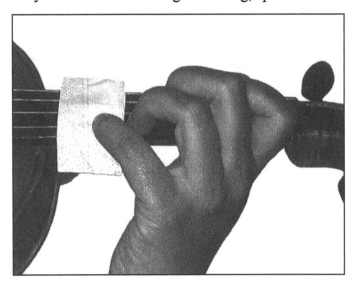

The round fourth finger

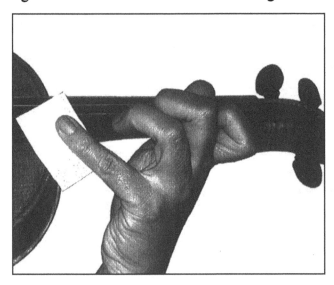

The long fourth finger

(Finger preparation without the bow)

2. The fourth finger extension without the intermediate step

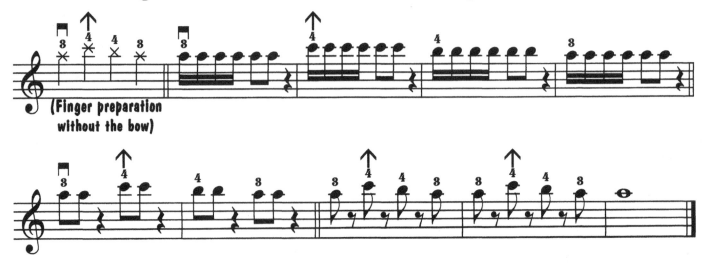

(Finger preparation without the bow)

3. Extension of the first finger backwards into the low position

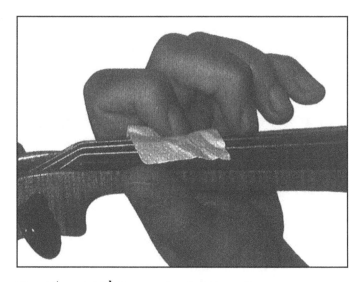

The 1ˢᵗ and 2ⁿᵈ fingers in the first finger pattern

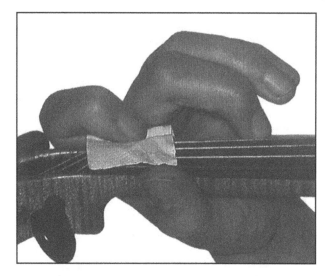

The 1ˢᵗ finger glides into the low position

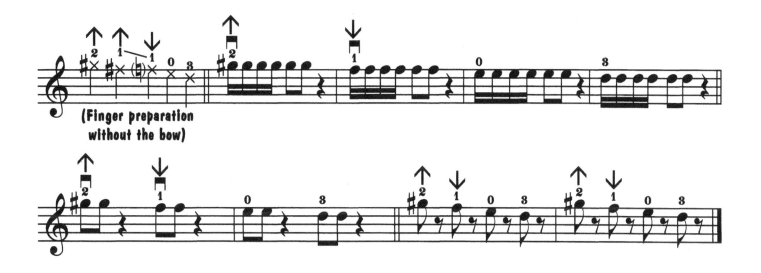

(Finger preparation without the bow)

⊙₂₈ **Hungarian Song**

Repeat three times!

37

Gavotte by Lully

⊙₂₉ **Your new piece – "Gavotte" by Lully**

Listen frequently to "Gavotte" while learning more exercises from the violin gymnastics section. But don't forget to periodically review the violin gymnastics in Book 2A.

The first three notes of the "Gavotte" – pizzicato as a model for a free and resonant tone

Pluck these three notes strongly. They should sound like a signal. Pluck the third note more strongly than the first two.

Using the pizzicato notes as an example, play these notes with the bow, striving for a clear tone beginning and a freely resonant sound.

The theme of the "Gavotte"

All musical phrases begin with broad, energetic strokes and end softly and gently. Begin the next phrase immediately with lots of temperament and let the signal sound: **"Let's go now!"**

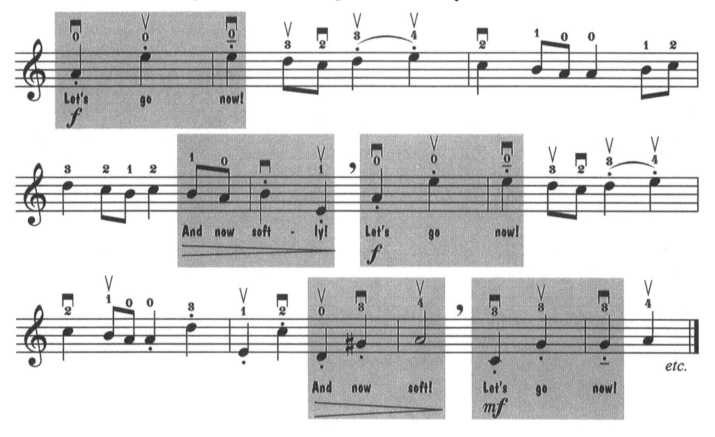

⊙₃₀ **Section A – in a slow practice tempo** (music on page 42)

The beginning of the middle section with short strokes

In the middle section of the "Gavotte" there are many difficult finger patterns. But have no fear, you have already practiced them in the "Hungarian Song." Study the photographs on pages 36 and 37 once more, review the sliding exercises, then play the beginning of the middle section slowly with short strokes. In the rest between notes you can prepare the next finger and place it in its correct place.

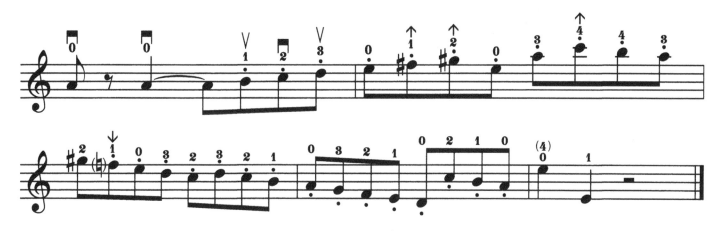

⊙₃₁ **Five ways to practice the beginning of the middle section**

The piano accompaniment on the recording can be used for all of the following exercises. Play a different rhythm each day. Which one do you like the best?

39

The Train Exercise

Imagine a train approaching from the distance. It gets louder and louder, roars past, then recedes into the distance.

Begin this exercise softly, bowing in the middle with **very little bow**. Get gradually louder by using more and more bow, then gradually get softer and return to the original volume.

In this exercise, it is not important to play the exact number of notes written. The goal is to execute the audible and visual volume and bow quantity changes.

The middle section with the crescendo and decrescendo

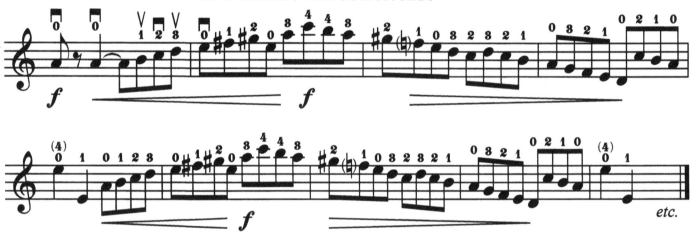

⊙₃₂ **Section B – in a slow practice tempo**   (Music on pages 42 and 43)

The transition to the middle section with a challenging bow scheme

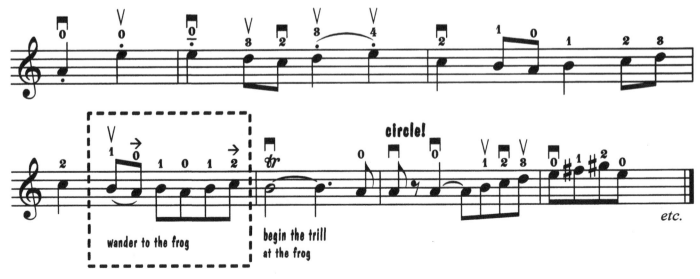

This is the first time we must play a real trill. Don't be frustrated if your trill finger is still a little sleepy. Tapping twice with the trill finger is a very good beginning! After the trill, stop on the first finger.

Six short trill exercises

Practice the following trill exercises regularly for the next few weeks. They will certainly increase the tempo, stamina and strength of your trill finger!

Maybe someday you will have a chance to hear the "Devil's Trill Sonata" by Tartini. This beautiful piece includes countless trills, indeed, even chains of trills. I am sure you will enjoy it!

33. "Gavotte" – **in a medium practice tempo** (Section A)
34. "Gavotte" – **in a medium practice tempo** (Section B to the end)

35. "Gavotte" – **in performance tempo** (Section A)
36. "Gavotte" – **in performance tempo** (Section B to the end)

J.B. Lully

Three preparatory exercises for the Wave Song

1. The elastic bow

Place the bow on the string at the balance point, hum the beginning of the Twinkle theme in ¾ time and flex the bow stick up and down. Do you feel the elasticity of the stick and hair?

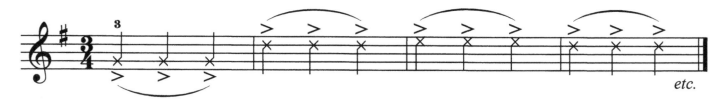

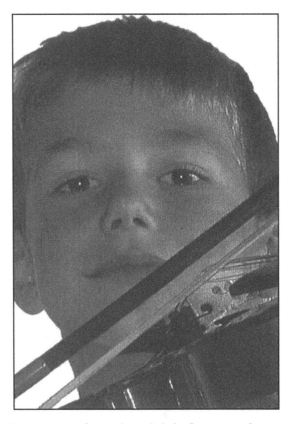

Do you see how the stick is far away from the hair in this photograph...

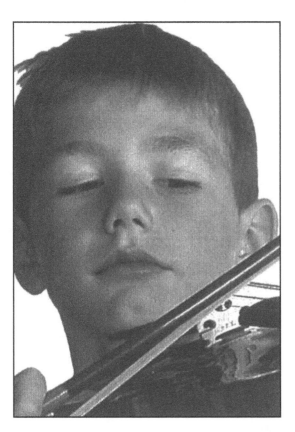

.... and almost touches the hair here?

2. Three tone waves on the open D string

Play the open D string very softly:

Now add three "waves" to this sound:

Pay attention to the following points:
- ♦ The bow should not stop but should move with a constant speed.
- ♦ The tone should not get scratchy during the "waves."

3. Dividing the bow into thirds

Divide your bow into three equal segments with chalk marks on the stick.

Measure 1: For each quarter note, use one third of the bow.
Measure 2: Use two thirds of the bow for the half note and one third for the quarter note.

At first, **stop** the bow between notes to verify that you are using the proper amount of bow. Can you stop the bow in the correct places with your eyes closed? Your mom or dad can tell you if you were successful.

When you have mastered the step above, bow as **evenly** as possible and give each note a **gentle wave** without stopping the bow.

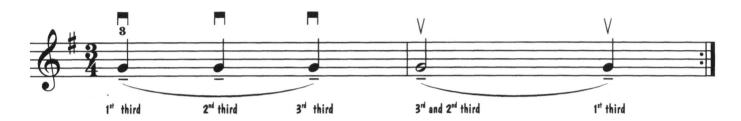

Wave Song

It could be that your first attempts at tone waves are somewhat clumsy. Learning this bow stroke requires lots of time and persistence. That is why we are beginning now. Think about how a simple caterpillar will one day develop into a beautiful butterfly…

Many years ago, this form of bowing was called "parlando" (meaning expressive or declamatory) because it emphasizes and accentuates individual notes so well – just as we emphasize words with our voice. In today's musical vocabulary this bowing form is called "portato."

Minuet by Beethoven

⊙ **38** **Your new piece – "Minuet" by Beethoven**

Listen to the "Minuet" frequently while doing exercises from the violin gymnastics section. Is the finger extension exercise becoming easier? Don't lose patience! It usually takes many weeks to master this motion.

Preparatory exercise for the beginning of the "Beethoven Minuet"

The beginning of the "Minuet" with three tone waves that get louder

1. Stop the bow after each down bow and check whether you have been successful in observing the following bow scheme:

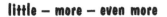

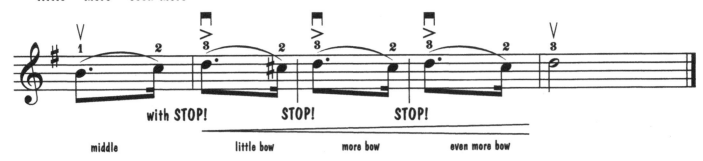

2. Play these measures again, this time without stopping the bow.

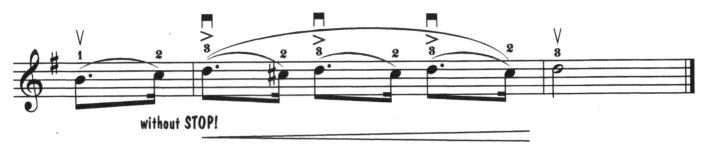

The first and second fingers in half position

As you move between the first and half positions, don't change your thumb or hand posture. Perform the position change using only a small forearm motion toward or away from the scroll.

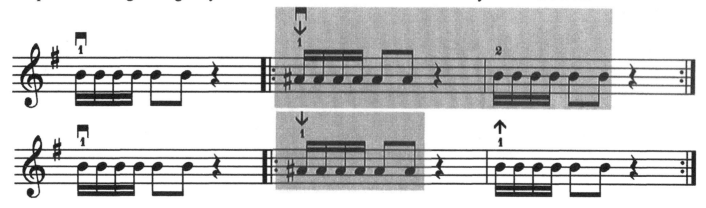

The half position in the "Beethoven Minuet"

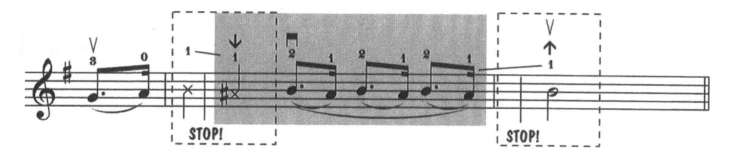

⊙₃₉ First part of the "Minuet" – in a slow practice tempo

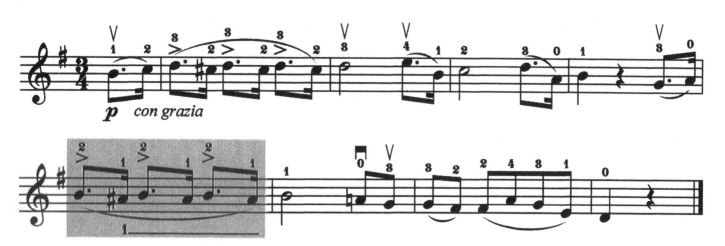

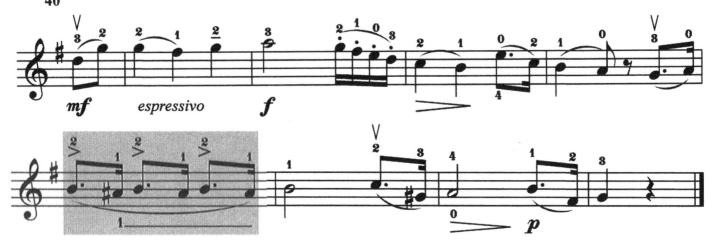

40 Second part of the "Minuet" – in a slow practice tempo

The half position in the "Trio"

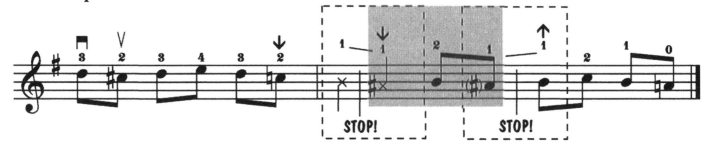

41 The G major scale with the Trio stroke

Play the up bows with a fast bow speed, stopping the bow distinctly between each note. Listen to the crisp tone start at the beginning of each note as well as the resonance after each note.

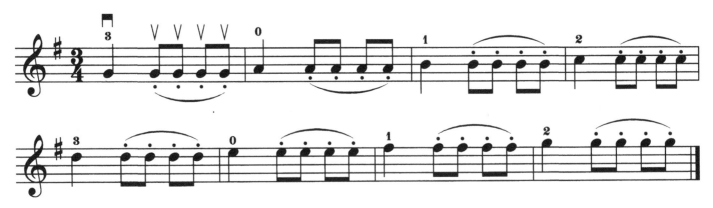

The beginning of the "Trio" with five string crossings in a row

Sliding the second finger

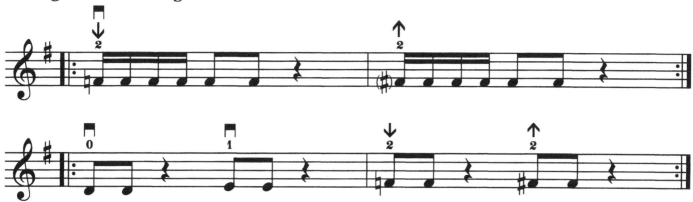

The passage in the "Trio" with the half step slide of the second finger

⊙ 42 First part of the "Trio" – in a slow practice tempo

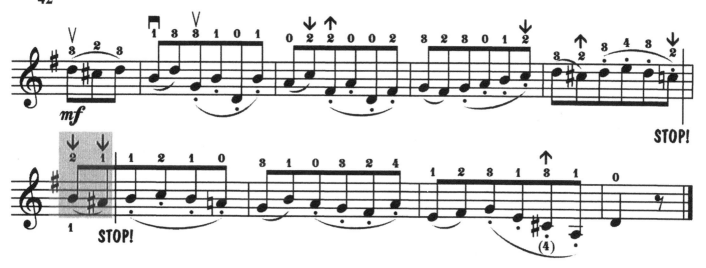

⊙ 43 Second part of the "Trio" – in a slow practice tempo

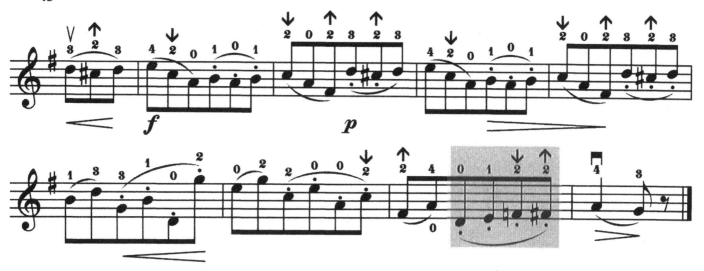

44. "Minuet" – medium practice tempo (Minuet)
45. "Minuet" – medium practice tempo (Trio to the end)
46. "Minuet" – in performance tempo (Minuet)
47. "Minuet" – in performance tempo (Trio to the end)

L. van Beethoven

Trio

Fine

D.C. al Fine

50

The A Major Scale: The calm before the storm

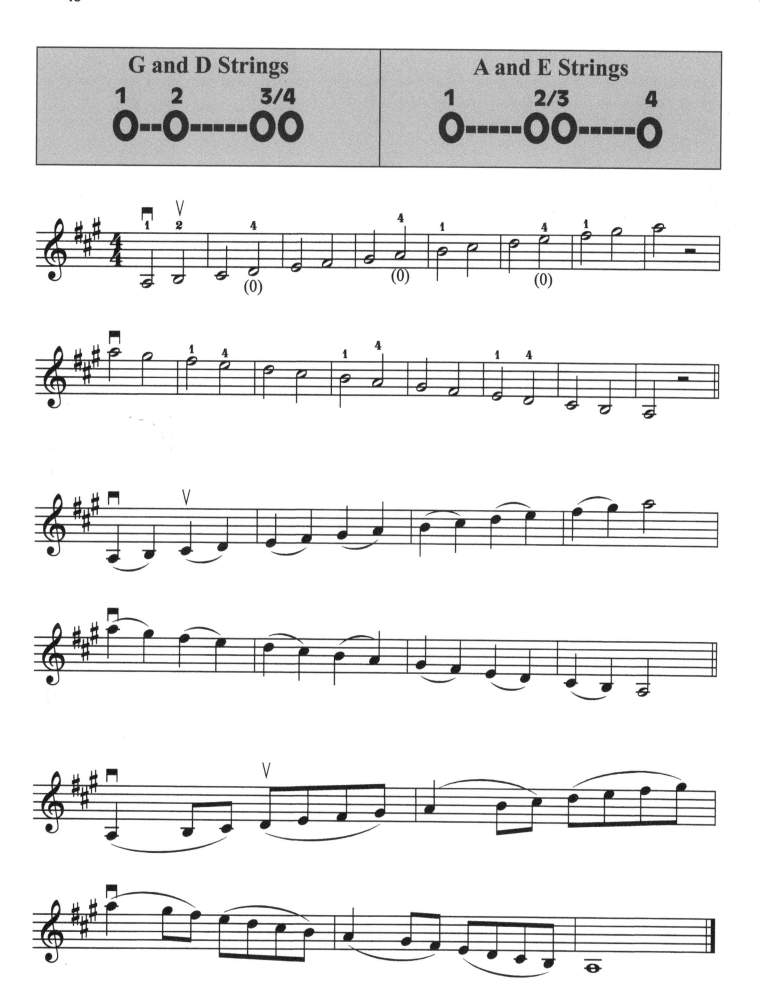

Preparatory Exercises for Shifting

Pizzicato exercise on all strings

In order to become familiar with different positions of the left arm, pluck the first Twinkle rhythm on all strings with the fourth finger of the left hand. Begin in the first position.

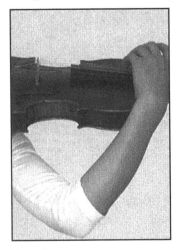

G string

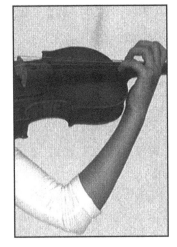

E string

Now play this exercise once more, but this time in the middle of the fingerboard. This corresponds to roughly the fourth position. Do you feel how your left hand touches the violin body in this high position?

First pluck this rhythm in the first position, then repeat the exercise in the fourth position.

+ symbol for *pizzicato* **using the left hand**

Pendulum Exercise

G string

Now, watch how your elbow can swing! When you pluck the E string, your elbow will swing far to the left. When you pluck the G string, you will see your elbow clearly on the right, as this girl is demonstrating.

Play the following exercise and use a flowing arm movement when you change strings.

First perform this exercise in the first position, then repeat it in the fourth position.

Harmonic or "flute" exercise

Here is how to make your "flute tone" sound beautiful:

- Instead of pushing your finger down on the string, let your fingertip touch the string very gently.

- Bow close to the bridge.

First position and the "flute tones" in sequence

The Happy Squirrel

Now your left hand should jump like a squirrel, naturally not from branch to branch but from one position to another! The audio accompaniment can be found on Volume 2A, Track 15.

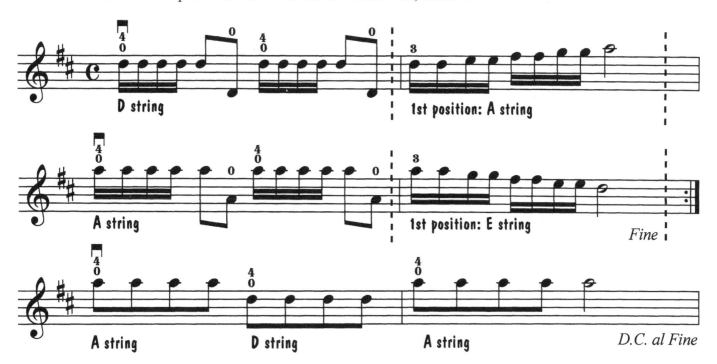

Minuet by Boccherini

⊙₄₉ **Your new piece - "Minuet" by Boccherini**

As you listen to your new piece, practice the exercises in the violin gymnastics section, especially the exercises from Book 2A.

The trill in the "Boccherini Minuet"

Now we will practice a trill with specific ornaments. It begins with the **upper note** and finishes with a **two-note ending**.

Bow all trill exercises with an accent at the beginning of the trill, but use a small amount of bow. The energy of your bow stroke will help activate your left fingers to trill quickly and strongly.

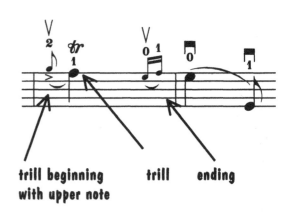

trill beginning with upper note   trill   ending

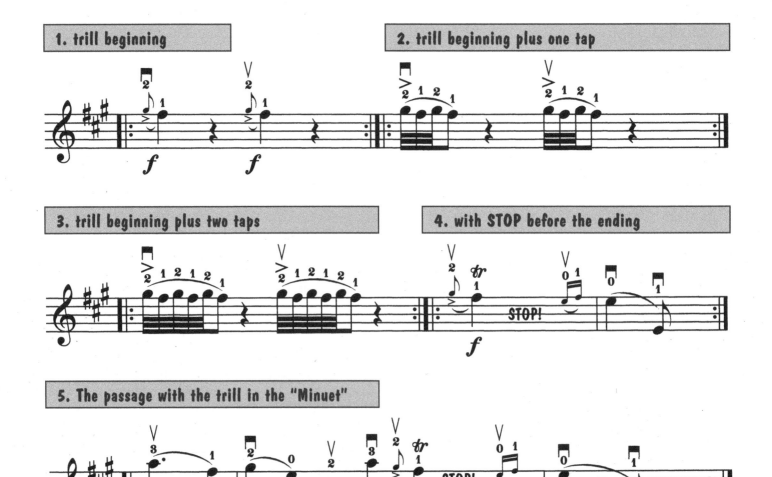

1. trill beginning

2. trill beginning plus one tap

3. trill beginning plus two taps

4. with STOP before the ending

5. The passage with the trill in the "Minuet"

slur - ring   slur - ring   up   down   trill   ending   down   down

The first measures in four small steps

First Step: The clear tone start in the upper half of the bow

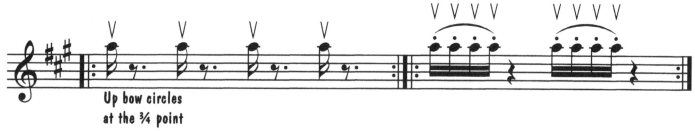

Up bow circles
at the ¾ point

Second Step: The beginning of the piece with staccato strokes

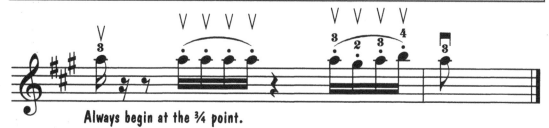

Always begin at the ¾ point.

Third Step: The fast, energetic strokes

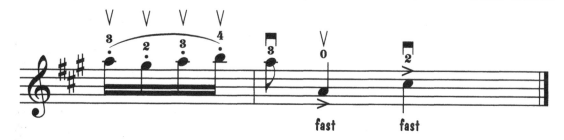

fast   fast

Fourth Step: The soft notes at the end of the phrase

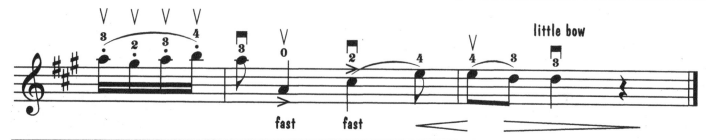

little bow

fast   fast

Fifth Step: The first two phrase together

fast   little bow   STOP!   fast   little bow

mf

clear
tone
beginning

The low fourth finger as an alternative to the high third finger

1. Preparatory exercise with the violin but without the bow

Place the third finger on the E string and place the fourth finger directly next to it. Hop with your fourth finger back and forth from the E to the A string. The third finger should remain in place on the E string.

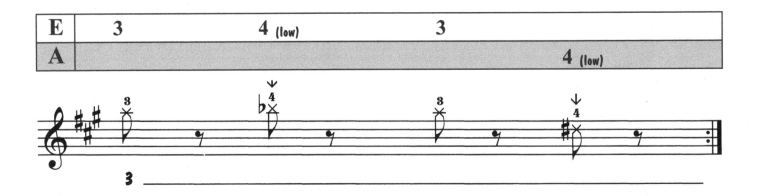

2. Preparatory exercise with the violin and bow

a. with the first Twinkle rhythm
b. with two short, separated strokes

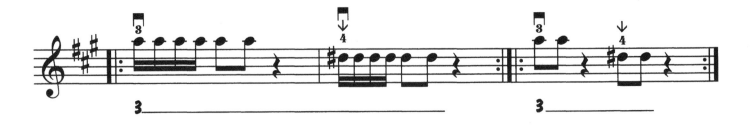

3. Preparatory exercises for this fingering in the "Minuet"

a. on the E and A strings
b. on the A and D strings

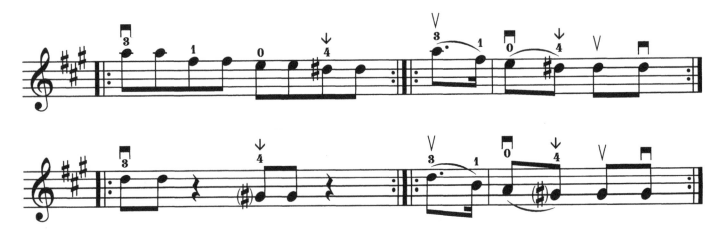

⊙ 50   "Minuet," first section – in a slow practice tempo

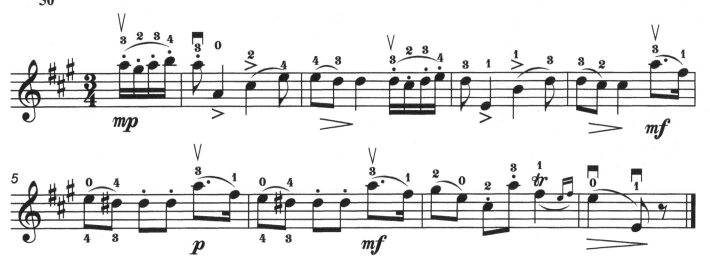

⊙ 51   "Minuet," second section – in a slow practice tempo

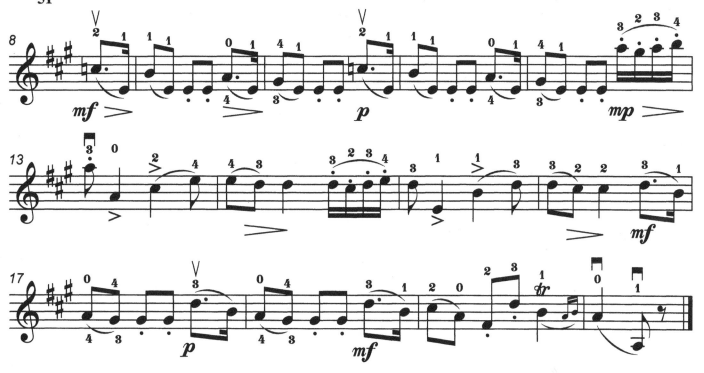

The crescendo eighth notes in the "Trio"

Preparatory exercise on the open D string

Begin by using very little bow in the middle and gradually use more and more bow. Stop the bow clearly between notes and listen to the beautiful resonance!

Preparatory exercise on the open D string   The corresponding passage in the "Trio"

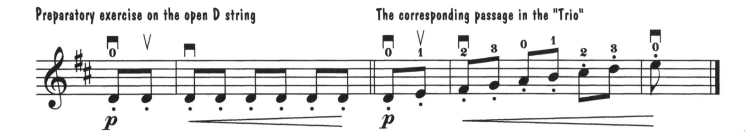

The quick placement of the fourth finger

The corresponding passage in the "Trio"

The decrescendo eighth notes in the "Trio"

Preparatory exercise on the open E string

Begin with energetic, broad strokes in the middle of the bow and gradually use less and less bow. Stop the bow clearly between notes and listen to the beautiful resonance!

⊙ 52 "Trio," first section – in a slow practice tempo

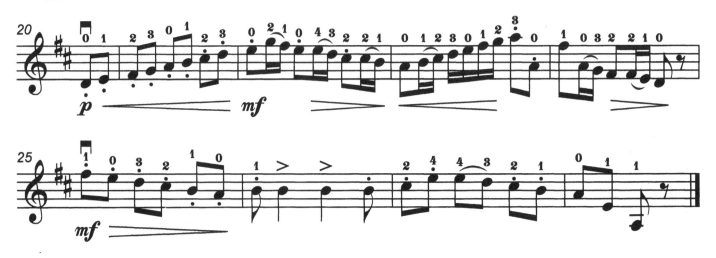

58

The "flute tones" in the "Trio"

In this passage, the roles have been switched: the violin has the accompaniment and the piano has the melody. Here is an arrangement for two violins that will help you to learn how the two parts fit together and when you should play.

53 "Trio," second section – in a slow practice tempo

54. "Minuet" – medium practice tempo (Minuet - first page)
55. "Minuet" – medium practice tempo (Trio to the end)
56. "Minuet" – in performance tempo (Minuet - first page)
57. "Minuet" – in performance tempo (Trio to the end)

L. Boccherini

Moderato e grazioso

Trio

D.C. al Fine

Congratulations!

**You have now completed Book 2B
and have beautiful pieces
by Martini, Bach, Dvořák and Becker awaiting you in Book 3.**

61

Progress Through Repetition

Dear parents, the subject of *review* was already discussed somewhat in the previous books. Now that your children are working in Book 2B or 3A, they will have learned a good number of pieces. To some parents and students, regular repetition of all pieces may now seem too laborious and complicated. Nevertheless, this area of practice should not be neglected. Regular review of high quality becomes ever more important as skill levels increase. What follows will illustrate both why review should not be neglected, as well as how to make it a fun and exciting experience.

What effect do review exercises have on children?

Children who regularly review previously learned pieces or learn new pieces and techniques through systematic repetition, gain fundamental experiences that can be applied to many areas of life. Musically their development is more advanced, and they have better command of their instrument than those who predominantly play only their current pieces. In order to illustrate some important aspects of review, try to imagine the following three scenarios:

First scenario: Think back to the time when your children made their first attempts to walk. They fell countless times, got back up, fell down again, scraped a knee and maybe cried. However, when they finally managed to walk a few steps, they would laugh with joy at their accomplishment. Untiring, they tried to walk again and again, alone or holding your hand. You remember these scenes very clearly.

Second scenario: We observe a circus performer balancing with confidence on the high wire, doing somersaults or jumping up and down. He stands smiling in the spotlight and accepts his applause. We all know how much intensive training and daily practice is required to perform such feats.

Third scenario: Imagine a beautifully well-groomed garden in full bloom. In the sunlight, under a tree, a monk sits peacefully and deeply absorbed in meditation. After a while, he stands up, picks up his bow and arrow, carefully takes aim, and hits the center of the bull's-eye.

The first scenario represents the natural need for learning and achievement found in small children, qualities that should be nurtured for life. The high-wire artist illustrates how much we can achieve when we constantly strive to improve ourselves, giving joy to others and gaining self-confidence in the process. The third scenario describes a path for inner development. Here, shooting with a bow and arrow serves as a means towards self-education. The monk isn't really interested in the handling of a bow and arrow. His objective can be found in the voluntary self-improvement revealed in his unwavering goal of perfect execution. A Zen saying clearly illustrates this principle:

> Whatever I do, I do whole-heartedly; I give my best.
> I do this naturally, with enterprise, joy and infinite care, playfully-serious

Why is it necessary to introduce systematic review exercises?

A. To learn new technical skills reliably
B. To refine and secure already-mastered technique
C. To elevate pieces already learned to a higher technical and musical level

What biological mechanisms take place in the brain?

Everything that is frequently repeated be it specific movements, isolated musical passages or entire pieces, creates new connections in the brain. With every further repetition, the neurons and synapses strengthen these connections. Now the brain is able to repeat these familiar actions with much less effort until they become almost automatic.

This process always occurs in the brain, whether it is a good or a bad habit. For this reason, it is extremely important to learn things correctly the first time. The *quality* of the repetition is of utmost importance, otherwise there is the danger that mistakes will be imprinted. The relearning of an incorrectly practiced motion pattern requires at least as many repetitions as were required to learn it wrongly in the first place. (see Frederic Vester "Denken, Lernen, Vergessen")

Why should review exercises be presented in an entertaining way?

Brain research tells us that people who link practice and learning in combination with joy and a pleasant atmosphere initiate a positive hormone reaction that leads to a smooth exchange between nerve cells. The successful completion of a task results in a sense of achievement that compels the student to apply himself even more and continue the effort.

How can you present review exercises to your child in an entertaining manner?

A. Suggestions for the practice of new technical skills or short, difficult passages

The practice pyramid

The student should practice the new technique or passage extremely slowly and carefully. When you are satisfied, he should try to play the exercise two times in a row without mistakes. Did he do it well? If not, he should go through the passage one time mentally or on his "magic violin" before trying it again two times on the instrument. When this is satisfactory, he can try to play the passage three times in a row, etc.

On the right is a drawing of a practice pyramid for a child who has played a passage ten times in a row without mistakes. There are a total of fifty-five X's, a truly fantastic achievement!

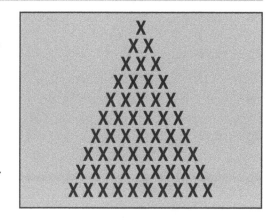

The Number Game

Your child picks a number between two and nine, which represents the number of times he believes that he can play a passage or exercise without mistakes. Then, he attempts to meet this goal. Was he correct with his prediction?

The Stairway Game

If you have stairs in your house or apartment, this game is lots of fun. Your child stands on the bottom step and plays the passage or exercise to be learned one or more times (depending on the length and difficulty of the passage). If he performs it well, he can take one step up and try the exercise again. As he progresses up the steps, he will certainly become more confident and proficient.

The Stepping Stone Game

This is much like the Stairway Game, except here the child begins next to a wall and takes steps forward when he performs well. When he does very well, he can take a big step. If only a small mistake occurs, he can take a tiny step. The game is over when he has reached the other side of the room.

B. Suggestions to improve and strengthen previously learned technical skills

All the games in Section A work well also for this area.

C. Suggestions to bring previously learned pieces to a higher musical and technical standard

The Sticker Game

Draw circles on a piece of paper and write the name of one piece to be practiced in each circle. Now cover each circle with a reusable sticker. Your child is allowed to remove one of the stickers and discover his task.

This game has the advantage of allowing you to plan the practice content precisely.

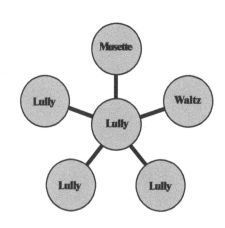

Exercise variations for the practice of new technical skills or short, difficult passages (Section A):
Write the numbers between two and nine in the circles and cover them with stickers. The number your child uncovers now represents the number of repetitions for the next exercise.

The Lottery Game

Through the Lottery Game, children become accustomed to regularly reviewing all of the previously learned pieces. The title of a piece or exercise should be written on each card and the cards collected in a small container. Every day, your child should draw a card, perform the piece or exercise, and then put the card in a second container. The cards should move from one box to the other within a predetermined length of time. This game is equally exciting for children, their parents, and their teachers, and it creates a happy and relaxed atmosphere.

Spin the Bottle

Lay cards with titles of review pieces or other exercises in a circle on the floor. (Examples: *Piece of choice with a beautiful tone, piece of choice with a beautiful bow hold,* etc.). Place an empty bottle in the middle of the circle. Now your child can spin the bottle and perform the piece or exercise to which the bottle points.

The Tree Game

Draw a large tree without leaves on a poster. Each time your child has repeated a piece and clearly improved its quality, he is allowed to draw a leaf on a branch or glue a real leaf in place.

Variation: Instead of a tree, you could draw a meadow or a flower vase on the poster. For each beautiful repetition, your child can draw a new flower.

More practice games

In the playroom, there are many aids that can help stimulate daily practice routines:

♦ Dominoes: For every well-performed practice activity, the child stands a domino on end in a row. When all review exercises have been completed, he is allowed to tip the first domino, starting a chain reaction.

♦ Legos®: When your child repeats a piece one or more times and demonstrates clear improvement, he is allowed to add a new Lego® to a house or tower. With time, he will be able to marvel at a masterpiece.

♦ Caravan: For each good repetition, a doll, model car or teddy bear can be added to a caravan.

♦ House of cards: With each successful repetition, a new section can be added.

♦ Paper chain: Each link in the chain represents a successful practice activity.

You can see that there are no limits to your imagination. Despite all the fun in these practice games, you should remember that your role is not that of an entertainer. Under your guidance, your child can collect fundamental experiences and develop characteristics that may have a lasting effect on his whole life: energy, continuity, sensitivity, self-confidence, self-assessment, and most importantly will power, patience and perseverance.

Dear parents, when you build these suggestions into your daily practice program, you will give your child much more than simply many hours of pleasant entertainment.

Golden Rules of Repetition:

1. **Practice correctly from the very beginning!**
   Strive to perform every repetion with great care and accuracy. You can only "reap" what you "sow."

2. **Concentrate fully on the task to be learned** and practice it so many times that you can play it confidently, indeed until you simply cannot play it wrong!

3. **Practice slowly at first so that you can play faster and with more confidence later on!**
   If you rarely or never practice slowly, you will certainly make many mistakes that you don't notice. Your mind can only follow along and prevent possible mistakes when you practice slowly and carefully.

4. **Divide a difficult task into several smaller tasks!**
   If a difficult passage doesn't imporve, divide it into smaller steps. They should be small enough so that they can be played with confidence in a slow tempo.

5. **Practice difficult passages with different rhythms!**
   Use different bowings or rhythms, practice slowly or quickly, softly or loudly, play sadly, thoughtfully or happily.

Notes

Notes

 Practice Plan

Theme this week:

Date:		1st day of practice	2nd day of practice	3rd day of practice	4th day of practice	5th day of practice	6th day of practice
1.	**Warm-up Exercise 1:** *finger pattern exercises (p. 15)*						
	Warm-up Exercise 2: *Let Us All Be Happy Now (p. 16)*						
	Warm-up Exercise 3: *The Bell Songs (p. 18)*						
	Warm-up Exercise 4:						
2.	**Violin Gymnastics with Music:**						
3.	**Exercises for your New Piece:**						
	New Piece:						
4.	**Review Piece with Specific Task:**						
	Other Review Pieces:						
5.	**Concert Piece:**						
6.	**Note-reading:**						

Place an X in the relevant box if you have practiced the task. How many X's will your practice plan have this week?

NEW!
Piano accompaniments to the STEP by STEP series available for download:

www.musicdownloaddirect.de